The Spiritual Traveler Vol. I

Cuba is a State of Mind

p.w. long

with

Juaquin Santiago and Elijo Truth

The Spiritual Traveler Series
provides the reader with a new type
of travel writing experience.

Instead of simply looking at the sights,
sounds, and tastes of a locale, the
Spiritual Traveler allows the reader to
experience the consciousness of a nation.

A tourist takes in the local sights;
a traveler sees the reality of a landscape.
- p.w. long -

The Spiritual Traveler Vol. I

Cuba is a State of Mind

p.w. long

with

Juaquin Santiago and Elijo Truth

blue ocean press
tokyo

1898 Consciousness Studies
Cuba - Puerto Rico - Guahan (Guam) - The Philippine Islands

Published by:

blue ocean press, an Imprint of Aoishima Research Institute (ARI)
#807-36 Lions Plaza Ebisu
3-25-3 Higashi, Shibuya-ku
Tokyo, Japan 150-0011

mail@aoishima-research.com
URL: http://www.thespiritualtraveler.com
         http://www.blueoceanpublishing.com
         http://www.aoishima-research.com

Cover Design by romeo carlos

ISBN: 978-4-902837-18-8

"Quien no tiene de Congo, tiene de Carabali"
(He who doesn't have Congo ancestry, has Carabali ancestry).
This is a Cuban saying illustrating the mixed blood heritage of the Cuban people. Congo and Carabali are two African nations from which people were taken to Cuba as slaves.

"Cognitive independence to act as active protagonists in our own history."
This phrase was stated by a Cuban educator (Rosa Maria Masson) to describe the essence of the Cuban spirit of independence and self-determination.

CONTENTS

Introduction –
CUBA IS A STATE OF MIND

What is it about Cuba that stimulates our senses, makes us yearn for more of her? What is the seemingly magical energy that permeates the soul of almost every Cuban? What is that infectious quality that can only be labeled "Cuban"?

If you truly allow yourself to partake of Cuba, sip from her cup, eat from her plate, take her in, you will never be the same. When you fully experience Cuba you must surrender. But once bitten, you cannot stay away, you must return. One thing is certain, you will not change Cuba—she will change you.

Cuba is that part of all of us that yearns to be free, to know and express our own power. Cuba is the manifestation of the ideal; she is the ultimate idea of the human potential. Cuba is a state of mind.

THE FIRST TIME I EVER SAW YOUR FACE

I was not disappointed. You were as beautiful and as sassy as I had imagined you to be. Seeing you for the first time actually took my breath away. I had waited some thirty odd years to lay my eyes on you and when I did, I walked along pinching myself to make sure I wasn't dreaming.

I had heard about your turbulent past, your wars of independence, your dictators, your mob connections, and flights from Miami transporting partygoers to the Tropicana. But I did not really take notice of you until the 1960s. Planes were being hijacked to your shores, Black Panthers were seeking refuge, and of course Fidel defied all political decorum when he stayed at the Hotel Theresa in Harlem and was said to have even sacrificed chickens. I was young and impressionable, and being so knew that I had to experience your glamour, intrigue, and bravado for myself.

For days, I felt like a five-year old at a carnival when I walked your streets. My heart pounded and my mind raced as my eyes tried to seek out every inch of you. Everything about you was new and exciting. I was swept up by your energy, your rhythm.

Girl, you are full of yourself—it shows, and I love it! I am impressed. You are free, self-assured, proud, and spirited. You are authentic, true to your beliefs and ideals. You are truly unique; there is no country like you. Endless struggle has made you wiser, stronger, and yes, more defiant. You are even more determined now than ever to defend your sovereignty. I know that I am smitten. I can't get you out of my mind, and I must see you again and again. Cuba, to know you is to love you!

NO PEASANTS HERE

My friend Anna works as a waitress in a Havana restaurant that caters to Cubans. Besides her job outside the home, Anna must meet the needs of her husband, teenaged daughter, and aging parents. Anna has a very busy life and, to my surprise when I asked what she did in her free time, she excitedly told me about the courses that she is taking by television. She is most proud to be learning English via the television.

Like most Cubans I have met, next to spirituality and family, Anna holds learning and getting an education in very high esteem. Cuba is probably the most educated society in the Western Hemisphere; Cubans seem to have developed to the extent that they are intrinsically motivated to learn, and value learning for the mere sake of learning. I find Cubans to be inquisitive and vigorous in seeking knowledge. Anyone who has ever engaged in intellectual banter with a Cuban will quickly discover that the myth often stated by Cuban exiles of Cubans being "brainwashed" is far from true. I dare say that Cubans are far more knowledgeable and critical in thinking than the majority of persons in the United States.

The Revolutionary government has accomplished the unthinkable. One of the significant successes of the Revolution has been the transformation of Cuba from a peasant society to a literate one in just 45 years. They have established a nearly literate nation. No other nation in history, not even the United States, has been able to accomplish this feat. Before the Revolution, ninety percent of the Cuban population was semi-literate or illiterate. Over half a million children had no schools to attend. There were few teachers, and those who did teach were out of work. The National Literacy Campaign of 1961 laid the groundwork for the education of a whole society rather than a privileged elite. Military barracks were converted into schools, a minimum of nine grades of schooling was ensured to all students and dozens of schools were established in remote areas, some serving only one to five students.

Today, education is free for all Cubans and the record of Cuban education is outstanding, despite severe economic constraints. The Cuban government and a cadre of dedicated teachers and administrators have created an educational system characterized by extensive school enrollment and attendance; widespread adult literacy; consistent pedagogical quality, and equal opportunities for all Cubans. Textbooks, notebooks, pencils, and all school materials are free of charge to students, and the state ensures that every student has a uniform and a meal at school. Cubans are extremely proud that the Constitution of the Cuban Republic guarantees no child or young person to be denied the right to an education.

Cuba has virtually become "one big university" since the government instituted the "Battle of Ideas," which makes university studies like the ones which my friend takes available to everyone. One of the most valued programs in Cuba is its educational response to unemployment. A new plan called the "Comprehensive Enhancement Program" treats study as a full-time job. The program was created for young people between the ages of seventeen and twenty-nine who were not in school and out of work. Now these young people study a range of subjects to raise their "general cultural level", prepare for a job and even a higher education.

Fidel was certainly on the right track, making the education of all Cubans a priority. Universal access to education has been used to stamp out social inequality. More than anything else, the Cuba of the over exploited and under educated peasant class is a thing of the past; the Revolution took care of that. Fidel maintains that "it is education alone that can save mankind." In his wisdom, he knows that an educated populace can never truly be oppressed. It has, in fact, been the exceptional education level of the Cuban people that has enabled them to persist in spite of very difficult circumstances. They will not be taken in by baubles, they know a good thing when they have it, and they are capable of discerning foreign propaganda from information of substance. Cuba may be considered "third world" in terms of its economy, but certainly it must be ranked as "first world" in terms of the knowledge, critical thinking, and attitudes of its people.

THE DAY THE GRANDMOTHERS RETURNED

On a sunny February day, I stood with hundreds of Cubans on Fifth Avenue in Havana, as they welcomed the grandmothers of Elián González home. As they passed, I too cheered and waved a Cuban flag. Elián González was the five-year old boy saved by the US Coast Guard after his mother and ten other people drowned when their boat sank en route from Cuba to Florida during Thanksgiving, in 1999. For three months, Elián had been kept in the United States against the wishes of his father, becoming the latest victim in the power struggle waged between the US and Cuba.

Ever since the decision was made to keep Elián in Miami, his picture was placed on posters in windows, on doors, and church altars. His name was reverently whispered by Cubans everywhere, and for at least four hours every day, Cuban television was devoted to the plight of this boy. The government organized "Free Elián" protests and summoned Cubans to attend nationwide rallies.

My colleagues and I, part of the US delegation to a conference of Cuban and North American educators, were as excited as the Cubans in anticipation of the grandmothers' motorcade. We felt extremely lucky, as the motorcade would come directly past Villa Eulalia, the teacher's hotel where we were housed.

As miniature flags were passed out to the crowd, emotions began to build. I could feel both a mixture of admiration for the grandmothers who had so nobly gone to the US to bring their grandson home, and an air of sadness because the journey had been in vain. A police escort announced the grandmothers' arrival, and we were told that the President was going to the General Assembly where the family would be honored. As the announcement was being made, Fidel's helicopter passed overhead.

The news media in the United States had often reported that the Cuban government organized the Elián rallies. On this afternoon I wanted to see for myself what part of the rally was orchestrated, and what were the true feelings of Cubans about the Elián issue. Were they happy that he had reached US shores and could now remain in the US or were they, in reality, unhappy that he was not allowed to return home to Cuba? I was astonished by what I saw that afternoon. As the grandmothers' motorcade passed, women cried and people spoke to each other of having faith in God that their precious *niño* would soon be returned. They questioned my colleagues and I as to why the government would want to keep a child away from the love of the father and his loving grandmothers. The women seemed unable to fully grasp or make sense of the situation. They could not believe anyone in his right mind would imagine a child to be better off without his family.

The anti-Castroites in Miami were confounded by Juan Miguel González's refusal to apply for asylum, by this affirmation of his wish to return Elián to "a nurturing life in Cuba." When Juan Miguel turned down offers of opulence—a home, money, and the opportunity for Elián to have constant exposure to Disney World, a debate ensued as to whether Elián would be better off in the Capitalist USA or in Socialist Cuba. Which country offered Elián the best quality of life? What, in fact, did Elian lose and gain by his father's decision to return him to Cuba?

To be sure, had Elián remained in the US he would have enjoyed an affluent life. He would most definitely have been the darling of the anti-Castro exile community and as such, would have enjoyed all the privileges that his defection would bring. He would probably have moved into a gated community, lived in lavish surroundings and never in his life, have to worry about money. He would have enjoyed celebrity status, as he now does in Cuba. In the US, he may have even become a child movie star, or the likes. He would probably have been given a hefty supply of Nike tennis shoes, Tommy Hilfiger shirts, and Playstation games to endorse. And of course, he would have become the official spokes child for Disney World.

Elián returned to a poor country, by economic standards. He returned to his home of Cárdenas, to a dilapidated town with potholed streets. Albeit a celebrity, but to a modest home in a neighborhood and not a gated community. Maybe Elián would keep some of the baubles his brief stay in the US earned him, but life in Cuba would be different. By bringing Elián home, Juan Miguel denied his son the wealth and material possessions that he would have obtained in the US. In Cuba, Elián will grow up understanding the value of the *libreta*, the ration book, and he will have only the luxuries that his father's working in the dollar (tourist) economy can provide.

But what did Juan Miguel give to Elián by bringing him back home to Cuba? Elián may be poor by the economic standards of the US, but certainly rich in terms of love, belonging, and security. Luckily, Elián was born into a culture where children are loved and indulged by their parents, families, and the government. Improving the lives of children continues to be a primary goal of the Revolutionary government. As with all Cuban children, Elián does not belong only to Juan Miguel. He is the nation's child. The day the grandmothers returned, love for all children of Cuba was reflected in the sadness and pleas of the women who lined the streets.

Children would never be allowed to go homeless or forced to sleep in cars, and worse yet, on the streets. Neither Cubans nor their government would stand for the physical abuse or sexual assault of their children. In the small county in which I live, five children were murdered by their own parents in one month. Many Cubans cannot even conceive of such an occurrence. I have ridden on city buses in Havana late at night and seen young girls on buses traveling about with no sense of fear while here in the US, young girls are kidnapped from their beds and snatched within two blocks of their homes. Cuban children go to school each day oblivious to the kind of dangers that students in the US must face, such as bullying, attacks, and mass murder. Columbine could not and would not happen in Cuba.

The experience of standing on the street that day greeting the grandmothers made me understand why the Cubans wanted Elián to come so badly, and why Juan Miguel did the only thing a Cuban father could have done. Juan Miguel traded all the money and the possessions he would have acquired to give Elián the things that really mattered. He brought Elián home to a loving, nurturing, and safe environment. Juan Miguel in his love and his wisdom made the right choice. He and the mothers who stood on the street that day believed Cuba was where Elián would receive the most precious gifts that a parent and a nation can give a child.

NO MORE DOLLARS

In a desperate move to attract hard currency, the Cuban government made the US dollar legal tender in 1993. This was primarily due to the fall of the Soviet Union and a significant loss of aid that followed. President Fidel Castro decreed on October 25, 2004 that, in the coming month of November, the island would no longer accept the US dollar in stores, hotels, and restaurants on the island, although dollar bank accounts would still be allowed. Cubans were encouraged to turn their dollars in or to save them. Banks swamped as 2.5 million people lined up to change their dollars and hundreds of thousands opened new accounts. While Cubans anxiously converted dollars into the newly converted pesos even tourists like myself, standing in a hotel currency exchange line, felt the tension. In a "self-determining" move, Fidel declared that "Cuba must be weaned off dollars to protect its economy and sovereignty from the economic warfare being waged by the US."

In recent months, the Bush Administration had taken harsh steps to stem the flow of US dollars into Cuba. The Administration had cracked down on US tourists visiting Cuba, had limited what Cubans living in the US could send to their families in Cuba (and in this process, redefining the meaning of "family") and had used fines and other forms of pressure to curb Cuba's ability to deposit dollars in international banks, thus limiting its ability to import goods. Detachment became a weapon in the economic and psychological warfare waged between Cuba and the US. The Cuban government considered switching to other currencies like the Euro as its only defense. After some 11 years, the Cuban economy would no longer have to depend on the currency of a country that considers it an enemy state. In this act of self-determination, detachment became a tool of empowerment, as separation from the dollar deprived the US of a weapon against Cuba.

Cuba's detachment from the US dollar will no doubt produce some tangible and intangible results for the Revolutionary government. Since my first trip to Cuba 5 years ago, I have seen the negative and not-so-subtle changes that dependency on the dollar has produced. To begin with, portraits of US presidents on the dollar were not only a mark of US dominance; they were also a constant reminder of white supremacy. By detaching from the dollar, Cubans would no longer be dependent on the very structure that epitomized that which they had waged a revolution to overcome; they would no longer deal in the currency that symbolized slavery and economic exploitation. Surely the Cuban sense of pride and esteem must well as they spend brightly colored notes with etchings memorializing their own revolutionary heroes like Ché Guevara, José Martí, and Antonio Maceo.

Since my first trip to Cuba five years ago, I have seen the negative and not-so-subtle changes that dependency on the dollar has produced. While happy to supplement their meager peso government salaries with dollars, many Cubans were angered by divisions the dollars were introducing into their relatively classless society. White Cubans were apt to have more access to dollars, as it was more likely that their families had emigrated to the US and were in a better position to send money back to Cuba, and Cuban society was again being divided along racial lines, something the Revolutionary government sought to change immediately after its takeover.

Of the black Cubans I talked to, most said their family members were not fairing well financially in the US, and several even suggested that their family members would return to Cuba if they could. These darker-skinned Cubans had not found in the US streets paved of gold or the promised land that they had anticipated. Upon reaching the dry earth of the US, they became black rather than Cuban, and as such faced similar to many other blacks in the US. With life being hard enough for darker-skinned Cubans in the US, they have been less able to send money back to families in Cuba. Members of what researcher John Ogbu terms "caste" minorities, the experience of dark-skinned Cubans were more similar to those of Puerto Ricans and Mexicans rather than that of light-skinned Cuban "voluntary" minorities. In fact, black Cubans did not find the early community of predominately white exiles to be of much help to them.

It is ironic that those most loyal to the government and the Party pay the highest price, in terms of exclusion from the dollar economy. In Cuba, the dollar has created a dual economy, and those with relatives in the US or those who earn dollars working the tourist sector live much better than those who depend on government salaries alone. In Cuba, one can easily see who is part of the new elite. Those with dollars to spend wear brand-name clothing and are able to buy the luxuries that a US currency affords.

When we took some Cuban friends to Casa de la Música to see a top Cuban musical group, I saw firsthand how access to the dollar excludes a majority of Cubans from the little luxuries of life. Tickets to the concert were, by Cuban standards, an unreal $25 per person, which cost us a whopping $175 for the evening. A typical bottle of rum, which costs $3 in the store, sold for $20 inside the club. Our friends thanked us profusely for the opportunity to attend the concert. They could never have attended, much less pay for their daughter to be there, since neither of them work in the dollar economy. As one ticket would have cost them a three-month salary, only privileged dollar holders or dates of dollar holders were able to attend a great "Cuban" event. The scene outside was pretty sad. A crowd of Cubans gathered behind a roped area, hoping and waiting for a tourist to take them inside to the concert as their "date." A Cuban friend was angered at the sight - thirteen and fourteen-year old girls who became the dates of adult European men for the evening.

The Revolutionary government has made the right decision to change to the new peso, in time to prevent another cultural revolution that would be detrimental to all for which Cuba stands. A self-determining people would never negotiate against their own economic interests or allow another country to set the standard for their economy, and in taking the steps that they did, the Cubans carried out what any self-respecting, self-determining, and self-valuing nation should. Cuba's shift away from the US dollar will stave off problems that dependency on the dollar will bring, such as race and class divisions, and hopefully slow the spread of moral decay.

It is said that "hungry people make poor shoppers." If Cuba had become a slave to the dollar, it would have eventually returned to the old days, and the Revolution would have been for naught. It was after all, the culture produced by the dollar that Cubans had rejected 45 years ago. Like other small countries the new peso has little use outside of Cuba. Maybe Cuba and other so-called "third world" countries, in the vein of self-interest, should levy a special tax on privileged "first world" tourists who can afford to enjoy the beauty and bounty of their environments. After all, why shouldn't those who have turned their own societies into polluted, crime-ridden, and stressed out environments pay plenty to enjoy their stay in a clean, safe and relaxed tropical island? "Third world" countries are fast becoming a desired commodity and those who come for leisurely pleasures should have to pay for it. If the name of the game is supply and demand, it makes economic sense.

WEARING CHÉ

While I sat through a timeshare spiel, the young salesman from Uruguay glanced and as if in disbelief, leaned over to examine more closely the medallion around my neck. "Ah! Ché," he said. "He's a good man." Our polite conversation immediately turned into something more personal, more warm, more engaging. His salesmanship turned to politics as he extolled the exploits of his hero. Although this encounter took place in the US, it reminded me of the very exuberant reactions I have received when wearing Ché in Cuba.

A large coin, Ché's image adorns the Cuban three-peso. It seems a befitting tribute to the man that so many Cubans idolize, and I have been astonished because it brings a constant response of absolute jubilation. It seems that everywhere I go, Cubans—saleswomen, tour guides, even customs agents take notice and express their pride and approval. In a hotel dining room, one waitress excitedly brought two others to see the medallion. As they politely asked permission to touch it, their faces were aglow with obvious pride.

Who is this person so revered by Cubans? Ché was a young man from a privileged background who in his own social transformation, chose to be involved in the international struggle against suffering of all forms. He abhorred most of all that which he considered to be needless suffering initiated by the greed of the ruling classes, and the contempt that they held for those who were poor and downtrodden.

Ché perceived man as an unfinished product capable of reaching a higher level of human function. He believed that the elimination of individualism was key to the transformation of society, that it was indeed possible for man to relinquish self for service to the community.

Ché was revered for his authenticity, he "walked the talk." In Ché, the Cuban people found one who was consistent in belief and action. With Ché, there was no hypocrisy; ideals were to be lived, not merely written on paper and quoted for political expediency. Ché maintained that the greatest joy a man could receive was in service to his fellow man. It was this total commitment to others and a profound love for humanity that has endeared him to the Cuban people.

Perhaps Ché, like Cuba, has become an idea in our minds. If so, what does he symbolize? What is Ché's concept of the "New Man" if not an expression of man's fulfillment? Ché realized what many of us have yet to even contemplate. He recognized the potential of man overcoming ego and connecting with his fellow man, utilizing his gifts for service to all mankind. He is cherished because he appeals to our desire to transcend our lower disposition, where disconnection from our brothers and sisters has led us to selfishly exploit them for our own interests. Ché represents the most human aspect in each of us that seeks to express our highest nature. Selfishness, greed, and the desire to dominate others are human defects that prevent us from tapping into higher aspects of ourselves, and those of us devoted to the good and service of humanity without the burden of selfishness and greed are answering the highest human calling.

There is an aspect of the transformed Ché in all of us. At our core, we know that to allow poverty, disease and ignorance to run rampant in the world is morally wrong. We know that it is obscene for the few of us to waste while the downtrodden majority struggles to attain the basic necessities of life. Maybe the "New Man" that Ché idealized is simply man and woman being reborn into true humanity.

THAT'S JUST THE WAY IT IS

Like many young blacks during the turbulent 60s, I was rebellious and impressionable. Black folks were torching stores, sniping from rooftops, shutting down cities, and now had the unmitigated gall to steal an airplane full of passengers. Those were the days! One of my fondest dreams at that time was to be lucky enough to board one of the jetliners that Brothers were taking to Cuba. "What daring," I thought: "the absolute audacity of a Black political outlaw to hijack an airliner to an outlaw nation!"

The rash of hijackings occurred at a time when black folks were just plain fed up and for once were starting to feel a sense of empowerment. They demonstrated the strength in a penny-box of matches and a gasoline-filled coke bottle.

The final stop for many of these political refugees was the outlaw nation of Cuba, and the number one outlaw in the eyes of the United States was none other than *El Jefe* himself. Ever since he dared to take his entourage to Harlem the tongues of black folks started wagging, and despite everything the US government said about Fidel, black folks saw him in a different light. The popularity that Fidel enjoys among black folks in the US also stems from his declaration that Black freedom fighters, otherwise known as thugs and criminals in the US, would be accepted and given status as political refugees.

A black man taking an airplane in the 1960s was a brave act, at a time when black folks were still being beaten and lynched in the South. Young blacks like myself admired the courage that the Brothers and Sisters exhibited. No, I didn't wish to remain in Cuba at the time, but I desired to take the ride and feel the power that was generated by the act. It was heady stuff just to think of touching the ground of a country that welcomed a black man.

There are supposed to be some 70-plus political exiles or refugees who are guests of the Cuban state. All of them are on FBI wanted lists and would face long years in prison or worse if they returned to the US. The very fact that they are in Cuba is a constant irritant in US-Cuban relations, and it is said that US diplomats routinely issue demands for their return.

It must be quite difficult to know that one's feet can never touch native soil again for fear of punishment or death. Never being able to see family or visit the place where the umbilical cord is buried wears on the soul of black folks. For these political refugees, this is it: It is Cuba or nothing. There are no options, and even if there were, perhaps the alternative of going home would not really be much of an alternative after all.

All this talk about what happens after Fidel dies must weigh heavily upon the minds of these Brothers and Sisters. They must wonder if their revolutionary comrades will continue to protect them a new regime will turn them over to US officials to curry political and economic favor. I have read and heard that among some of these refugees is a sense that the Revolutionary government betrayed them because it did not aid the armed struggle occurring in the US during the 1960s. Others are angry and frustrated by the racism that they see in the post-revolutionary racial utopia. Despite it all, however, Fidel retains his revolutionary integrity. They were his comrades in the larger struggle, and this kinship is the silver cord that connects them to Cuba and ultimately protects them. He has not betrayed their trust by turning them over to US authorities.

Everything and yet nothing has changed in the forty-odd years of their exile. The racist, materialist, oppressive mentality that these refugees fought against remains strong as ever, although perhaps it is being practiced in different venues. J. Edgar Hoover vowed that there would never again be another movement among young black men like the Panther Party, and he was right. The Black boys who would have stepped up to protect the Community as young men and women before them had done now selfishly destroy their own people. The occupation of choice is drug dealing, which contributes to at least 1/3 of them being attached in some way to the criminal justice system—either in jail, prison, or on parole.

Unlike those who came before, many of today's young black males could not read revolutionary literature if their lives depended upon it. Rather than becoming educated to lead their people, too many black boys are often suspended, expelled, or just plain dropouts. Pawns in the game, they can't read, can't think, and are like sheep going to slaughter. Many of those who do make it don't look back. Too many consider being black a burden, and helping out other black folks to be an even bigger one. They now want to live large have a 6,000 square-foot house in a gated community, drive an SUV, and wear bling. Making it in the materialistic, consumerist world is the struggle that they are committed to.

If the Black political refugees from the 60s should ever come back, it would not be home. The home they long for exists only in the mind, just as the home that Cuban exiles in the US cling to exists only in their minds. The place of struggle where young men and women changed things, where consciousness was raised, where the playing ground was leveled and all people experienced equality does not exist. Life in Cuba has not been easy for these refugees, but nothing they have endured in Cuba compares to what they would face in a US prison. Cuba offered them a second chance at some semblance of the idealized life of which they dreamed. Life in Cuba has not been perfect but at least it was a chance at life. Their home in the US does not exist anymore. Perhaps it does not exist in Cuba either, but Cuba is as close as they will ever get to realizing their revolutionary ideals, "that's just the way it is."

THE LEGACY OF SLAVERY

Slavery left an ugly mark everywhere it occurred: disenfranchisement, economic exploitation, and inevitable racism based on the ideology of white supremacy. It is amusing to hear Cuban exiles in Miami speak of racism not existing in Cuba, or punctuating their remarks with empty affirmations such as "a black doctor lived next door to us in Miramar." It is equally interesting to hear Cubans living in Cuba proclaim that racism to be a thing of the past, "the Revolution took care of that." To the credit of Fidel and the Revolutionary government, state sanctioned racism has been virtually eliminated.

No, the faces of black Cubans are not as visible in the upper echelons of government or on beloved Cuban television soap operas. Black Cubans will tell you that they are stopped more often by the police and watched more closely when they enter a tourist hotel. Some US blacks that fled to Cuba during the 1960s are understandably disenchanted with the current state of race relations in Cuba. Why then will most Cubans, even black Cubans, say that racism is a non-issue in Cuba? The answer might lie in perceptions of the vast difference between life for dark skinned Cubans before and after the Revolution.

After slavery in Cuba ended in 1886, black Cubans were still marginalized politically, socially, and economically. But with the occupation of Cuba by the United States from 1898 to 1902, the US form of racism was introduced into Cuba. The efforts of black Cubans in the struggle against Spain were minimized, black officers were belittled, and blacks were made to assume a subservient position in the "new Cuba".

Though they were instrumental in winning the war for Cuban Independence, US-style racism brought "Jim Crow" which meant separate and unequal schools and facilities for black Cubans, relegation to menial jobs with the lowest pay, and second-class citizenship. Older black Cubans tell stories reminiscent of the old South, like having to get off the sidewalks when white Cubans passed. This treatment of black Cubans continued up until the Revolution.

One of the first acts of Fidel was to state that Cuba would be a racism-free country. The government immediately outlawed institutional racism while acknowledging that it would take time for personal attitudes to change. It would appear that the Revolutionary government's desire to make the Revolution successful has helped Cubans transcend some racial attitudes carried over from slavery many of which are still prevalent in the US. One such attitude that has persisted in the US since the enslavement of Africans is the myth of the intellectual inferiority of blacks. These beliefs were enforced from the late 1890s through the1920s with so-called "scientific" studies, which supposedly provided evidence that the intelligence of blacks was lower than that of whites. Even today these viewpoints persist, and contribute to what is called the "achievement gap" in the US. Cuba does not have a racial achievement gap; in fact, Cuba boasts a 98% literacy rate. The literacy rate alone is testament to the fact that at least in education, institutional racism has been eliminated.

Cuba is not racism-free, it may never be, as is the legacy of slavery. Long after the chains have been banished, the ugliness of the brutal system remains. Nations like individuals reap what they sow; nations that benefited from the cruel institution of slavery will have to deal with and eliminate its remnants—exploitation, discrimination prejudice, and racism. The abolishment of institutional racism is a major step in creating a free, just, and democratic society. Two US educators have stated that the first step in achieving equality in the US is to reduce the racial achievement gap. It looks as if Cuba, despite scarce resources, has taken a major step toward eradicating racism in its society.

The more one delves into the issue of racism in Cuba, the more it becomes apparent that perhaps Fidel's greatest crime was not making Cuba a socialist island but opening the doors of opportunity to black Cubans. Perhaps Fidel's greatest mistake in regard to race was to refer to Cubans not merely as Latin Americans but as Latin Africans, and to concede that more than 60% of all Cubans have African Blood. This single act alone earned him disdain and hatred. One great dame in exile said that he (Fidel) was responsible "for bringing the monkeys out of the trees and putting them into the government," of course by implication spoiling Cuba, the Cuba that was dear to her.

It seems the greatest fear of the old Cuban aristocracy is that Cuba may one day become another Haiti. During the 1870s, Spaniards were imported from Spain to ensure the demographic dominance of white Cubans. Those in power declared that Cuba would never become a black republic and set about relegating black Cubans to a lower caste. With these prevailing attitudes one must wonder if racism is what truly lies at the center of the US blockade on Cuba.

"JUST THINK WHAT HAITI COULD HAVE BEEN"

A few years ago, I had the occasion to take a taxi driven by a Haitian immigrant. Over the course of my half-hour ride, we covered a variety of topics, including his emigration to the US and the future of his country. While he was making a good life for himself and his family in the US, he was saddened by the events taking place in his country. He lamented that Haiti was doomed. His next statement thoroughly surprised me. "You know, Papa Doc and Fidel came into power at almost the same time," he said. "Papa Doc in 1957 and Fidel in 1959. If Papa Doc had been the man that Fidel is, Haiti would have been so far along by now. Just think what Haiti could have been."

Some 40 years after that decisive moment in history, Cuba and Haiti are worlds apart and the men who came to lead them at decisive moments in history made all the difference. Francois Duvalier or "Papa Doc" as he was known, and Fidel Castro Ruz guided their countries in two very different directions and will leave very different legacies. Fidel was able to turn a peasant nation into one of the most literate nations in the Western Hemisphere. Papa Doc was a man so greedy and power-hungry that he managed to bring an already poor nation into a state of unimaginable poverty and misery.

When Duvalier took power in 1957, the small mulatto ruling class (5% of the population) pillaged the nation while black peasants became poorer and more desperate. Duvalier's focus was on the privileged few, maintaining power, and accumulating vast sums of money, all with the okay of the United States. Since the days of Papa Doc, the island has been plagued by political violence. It is a major Caribbean transshipment point for cocaine en route to the United States and Europe, as well as a center for substantial money laundering activities. With its beggar status and need for foreign intervention, Haiti can surely not be considered an independent, sovereign nation.

Haiti—the first black republic in the Western Hemisphere, a nation so full of hope and promise—is the poorest in the Western

Hemisphere. Papa Doc's land reforms confiscated peasant land holdings, allotting them instead to TonTon Macoute bigwigs while the miserable slums of Port-au-Prince swelled with homeless. 3/4 of the Haitian population is illiterate. 80% of the population lives in abject poverty. Haiti, almost 50 years after Duvalier assumed power, has a life expectancy of 53 years. The infant mortality rate in Haiti is 73 deaths per 1,000 live births. In 2004, civil strife and extensive damage from flooding in the Southern end of the island further impoverished the nation. Malnutrition and famine have become commonplace, even though many Haitians work for foreign companies. Women go hungry as they make baseballs for a mere five cents per hour working in toxic conditions. Persistently troubled by government instability, civil unrest, near-anarchy, Haiti has not yet attained true sovereignty.

During the time of Batista's deposal by Fidel's Revolutionary Army in 1959, foreign individuals and foreign companies owned 75% of all farmable land in Cuba. The new government confiscated much of the property of the foreign companies and adopted land reform. Land was turned over to landless peasants and farmers were able to join their land in farm cooperatives. After Fidel's rise to power in 1959, just the opposite occurred. The peasant class was eliminated, land was redistributed, and universal education and health care were made a priority. The economic egalitarianism established by Fidel is still evident in Cuba today. While all Cubans have had to share the pain of the Special Period, at the same time, all Cubans have maintained their right to health care, education, housing and food rations.

At the time that Fidel assumed power, a quarter of Cuba's population was illiterate, most of them residing in the countryside. The first great initiative of the Castro regime was a literacy campaign. Fidel considered education to be a basic right of all Cubans and encouraged this right in the national constitution. Today, Cuba enjoys a ninety-eight percent literacy rate, one of the highest in the world. A 1998 UNESCO assessment of educational achievement in Latin America rated Cuban students far above their peers in other nations in the region.

The loss of Soviet aid to Cuba and the Helms-Burton Act, resulted in Cubans going hungry between 1989 and 1993. The decline in food production led to an estimated 30 percent drop in caloric intake in the early 90s and the average daily per capita protein consumption dropped by 27 percent. During the worst years, Cubans suffered from diseases caused by malnutrition, but Cubans never suffered wholesale famine. Today however, Cuba is notable for the national organic agriculture initiative undertaken in order to feed a population faced with starvation. Under Fidel's leadership Cuba restructured its agricultural industry, focused its scientific efforts on organic solutions, and as a result rapidly and successfully feeds its people entirely by organic production.

According to UNICEF, Cuba is one of the seventeen countries that have the lowest indices in the world for the mortality of children older than one year of age. During the 1993-1995 period, considered the worst in Cuban history, the infant mortality rate was 10 for every 1,000 live births. By 2002, the rate was only 6.5 per every 1,000 live births.

Prior to 1959, the life expectancy in Cuba was 59 years; today the life expectancy of Cubans is 76 years. This factor is the result of a policy of providing universal health care to the people. Through Fidel's leadership, large amounts of money have been earmarked for social purposes, countless doctors and paramedical personnel have been trained, research institutes have been created, and hospitals built in even isolated parts of the country. Cuba's life expectancy has been achieved in spite of the blockade that attempts to prevent Cuba from obtaining medicines and medical equipment.

The taxi driver's comments have raised some questions in my mind, if only rhetorical. What if Duvalier instituted a land reform program that eliminated the peasant class? What if rather than appeasing the mulatto ruling class Duvalier had made his goal that of equalizing Haitian society? What if Duvalier had believed that universal education, health care, and decent housing was the right of all Haitians rather than a privileged few? What if Duvalier had refused to let foreign companies continue to exploit the labor of his people and his country's resources? What if Duvalier loved his people more than money and power? What if Duvalier had loved Haiti the way that Fidel loves Cuba? What could Haiti have become?

THE SPIRIT OF MACEO

It is rumored that the fourth person in line to ascend to the leadership of Cuba is a black man. So if by some karmic twist, Fidel, Raul, and president of the Cuban Parliament Ricardo Alarcón, all died, then a black general (perhaps Antonio Maceo incarnated) would "rule" the country and bring to fruition the greatest fear of early Cuban loyalists.

Antonio Maceo, the great general and hero of the Cuban Wars of Independence, was as close as Cuba ever came to having a black leader. Known as the "Bronze Titan," he was a mulatto of mixed African and Spanish descent who hailed from Santiago and rose from the ranks of private to general in the rebel army during the First War of Independence (1868-1878). Maceo was a constant source of political controversy. His foes were especially concerned about the emergence of a black man to a position of importance and leadership, and he suffered insult and criticism because he was a man of color.

During both wars for Cuban independence, the Spaniards capitalized on the racist attitudes of white Cubans and fueled their fears of a black-dominated Cuba comparable to the Republic of Haiti. Maceo's enemies spread malicious rumors about his so-called secret ambitions insinuating that Maceo was waiting for an opportunity to lead black soldiers against whites for the seize of power, and that he was favoring black officers over whites. A pamphlet published in the US implied that Maceo saw himself as the spokesman for black Cubans and that his goal was to establish the dominance of the black race in an independent Cuba. Ultimately, these rumors were ultimately a factor in undermining the unity of the Cuban insurgency.

Even while his foes sought to undermine his position, Maceo continued to fight for a free Cuba for all Cubans. In a spirit of resolution and defiance, he opposed all who tried to use the race card to destroy the revolution. While he embodied the hopes of blacks in Cuba, Maceo believed that there were no white Cubans, no black Cubans; there were only Cubans, and all should work together to establish a free republic.

Ché Guevara declared Maceo to be the "greatest of revolutionary guerilla fighters," and lauded his courage in continuing to fight for Cuban independence alone, despite almost impossible odds. He extolled the spirit of Antonio Maceo as the spirit of Cuba: "His act of courage and defiance in rejecting the Treaty of Zanjón (minor political concessions of the Spanish to end the First War of Independence) has made Maceo an enduring hero to generations of Cubans."

The symbol of a free Cuba, Maceo was a model and inspiration for freedom fighters during the Revolution of 1959. He never betrayed the Revolution's goal of fighting imperialism and promoting social justice and human responsibility. Like Maceo, Cubans embody the will to sacrifice everything to the cause of a free, autonomous nation. Like him, they are defiant, resolute, and determined to fight until the end to ensure Cuba's sovereignty.

TWO CUBAS

I drifted into Little Havana in Miami not so long ago. Actually, that's not quite accurate. I went to Little Havana to find a good guava pastry and a real *café con leche*, not a "latte." This little act proved to be truly enlightening as I had the opportunity to talk with Cuban exiles and hear their perceptions of Cuba.

Cuban exiles love Cuba. They love the idea of what they knew, what they have been told, and what they left behind. I met and talked with the daughter of one of those exiles who herself left when she was but four years of age. What seemed almost surreal was that she talked about Cuba as if she had recently arrived in the US, and had come only for a short visit. She knew everything of this place, minute details about the Cuba that she and her parents had left some forty years ago. She collected everything she could put her hands on about present-day Cuba, but psychologically kept it all in the compartment of "Cuba past". I have met many Cubans like her in exile. So many, that by the time I left I felt I was in a time warp. What makes the experience most interesting is that nearly two months before, I had heard the story of a different Cuba told with the same level of intensity. So here I was, trying to process these two completely different and competing views of one Cuba.

The Cuba that my exiled friend left was a splendid place. It was a tropical island with unlimited sun and sand. By Latin American standards, Cuba of the 1950s was an urbanized nation with a large middle class and a high income per capita. My friend's families lived well; they came to Miami for vacations and shopped in stores for imported products and luxury items. They were educated in private schools, had servants, and lived comfortable lives.

The Cuba of my friend's parents was a tropical playground for foreign tourists, US businessmen, and financers. It was a hangout for US mobsters by the likes of Meyer Lansky. Planeloads of partygoers would come from Miami to have fun at the famous Tropicana. They danced to the rhythm of the rumba, mamba, and cha-cha-cha. They enjoyed the casinos and nightclubs. Men fulfilled sexual fantasies through easy access to voluptuous Cuban prostitutes.

The other Cuba, I hear, was quite different. Before the Revolution of 1959, life was not easy. In fact, for most Cubans life was exceedingly hard. On the eve of the Revolution 700,000 Cubans were out of work; 500,000 farm laborers nearly starved, able to work only four months of the year; 100,000 small farmers labored on land that was not theirs; and 200,000 peasant families had no land on which to cultivate food. In this other Cuba, a large sector of the population suffered from hunger and malnutrition. They experienced extreme poverty, poor housing, high infant mortality, illiteracy, and disease. And while some Cubans lived a life of luxury, the majority lived in abject misery.

Prior to the Revolution, women fared especially poor in this other Cuba. A majority of women, poor and working class (17% of the workforce) were faced with limited opportunities of employment. Seventy percent of these women worked as domestic servants in the homes of wealthy white Cuban women. They worked long hours under oppressive conditions, lacking fringe benefits, and receiving miserable pay.

In this Cuba, aside from domestic servitude, the second largest area of employment open to women was prostitution. Young women who did not want to work as maids, migrating to cities from the countryside were forced to cater to the sexual whims of US tourists, businessmen and military personnel, and even wealthy Cuban men.

Black Cubans in pre-Revolutionary Cuba fared especially poor, which might explain their seemingly enduring support for Fidel and the Revolution. Black Cubans faced discrimination similar to that of the US South: discrimination in schooling, employment, and public services.

Most interesting are the comments about the Special Period. No one I know in Cuba has ever said or pretended that life there was easy. *No es fácil* is the constant refrain, but they have said with certainty that even the Special Period is better than what they were forced to endure before the Revolution. The Special Period has even been described as magnificent in comparison to pre-revolutionary Cuba.

It is understandable why Cubans in exile can never let go of the Cuba they knew. Life was exceedingly good. It is also understandable why they want to return and take up where life left off. Who doesn't appreciate and desire the good life? It is clear why Cubans who have remained in Cuba have endured and continue to endure the worst of deprivation, promising a fight to the death if it means that they will never have to go back to the Cuba they knew prior to the Revolution. Even with the hard times, a majority of Cubans today find the reality of present-day Cuba, despite the hardships, preferable to the memory of the old one. Two Cubas, seen through different eyes, experienced in grossly different ways - one through the eyes of exiles, and one through the eyes of those who stayed behind.

TRUE BELIEVERS AND NON-BELIEVERS

There currently exists a generation gap between those who experienced life before the Revolution and those born after it, which has become a greater problem to the true believers than the Special Period. Despite political education by the state, cracks are appearing in the consciousness of Cuban youth. Unlike their parents who espouse communalism, collectivism, purpose and service for the good of all, many of today's Cuban youth are dazzled by the materialism that pass through the airwaves or arrive in suitcases from Miami. Children of true believers in the Revolution have become believers in individualism. They want the things that dollars can buy. They want to visit Disney World like Elián, drive a fancy car, and live in a high rise along Brickell Avenue in Miami. They want the "good life" and they no longer believe that it can be found in Cuba.

On one occasion my friend Sonia asked me to speak with her son, who has become rebellious. She and her husband, true believers in the Revolution, do not understand him and can no longer communicate with him. He wants things—name-brand sneakers and hip clothes from the US. All he talks about is the "good life" there. Sonia insists that I speak with him, tell him the reality of life in the US, especially for blacks and the poor. She and her husband are trying to prevent the unthinkable, a fear that one day her one and only son will slip away illegally to the US and they will never see him again.

The "unthinkable" did happen to a high school professor that we met. In great pain, he recounted how his daughter had illegally fled to the US. With a mix of great sorrow and anger, he wonders why she would do such a thing. "She had everything here," he insists, "why would she leave?" By Special Period standards, his daughter was fortunate. She lived in a modern apartment in Miramar, a residential seaside area previously reserved for wealthy white Cubans. The Professor hears from his daughter, now distraught and disappointed and unable to return to Cuba. "I have lost my daughter," he says, and asks that we come to his classes and talk to his students. "Tell them what they will give up if they leave Cuba," he pleads.

Cuba is slowly being divided into believers and non-believers. Despite the hardships of the Special Period, the generations who lived through the Revolution and tasted its immediate fruits have become true believers. They know what life was like before. They felt the power of the people, overthrowing the brutal dictatorship of Batista and wrestling their country from foreign intrusion and exploitation. They are proud, defiant people who believe they are better off now despite the trials and tribulations experienced during the Special Period. The true believer will fight to the death to ensure that Cuba remains a sovereign nation.

The post-Revolution youth of Cuba are similar to the post-Civil Rights generation of African American youth in the United States. They are the beneficiaries of great privileges that they take for granted. They only read about the struggles that those before them experienced. They have no idea of the pain, punishment, imprisonment and even death that earned them the right to lives that they now enjoy. Cuban youth should never take the free housing, education, and healthcare for granted, just as African American youth must never take the right to vote or the right to go to a public facility for granted, because of the high price that was paid to earn them that right.

The non-believers are too young to know of the time when more babies died in Cuba than were born, or when the poor were excluded from treatable diseases because they had no money to pay a doctor. The non-believers dream of fancy houses in Miami, but are unaware of the time when the majority of Cubans lived in miserable shacks and entered decent housing only as domestics. They hear the stories from their parents of the days when a child of the working-class poor could not even dream of reaching a higher status in Cuba, but listen with disbelief. Many of these non-believers are too young and impertinent to realize the privilege of getting a free education from elementary to college without the worries of paying off years of student loans. They have no concept of the US system, of low expectations held by teachers, of suspension or expulsion from school, because the Cuban constitution guarantees their right to a free education. The youth do not think of these things; because they have only known the benefits of the Revolution, they cannot even fathom what life was like before.

The grass always seems greener on the other side, especially in the face of effective propaganda. Youth are naturally drawn to the bright lights and bauble - that is the weakness of youthfulness; they lack the wisdom to see beyond glitter. Most will not listen and unfortunately will have to learn the hard way. Many Cuban youth who defy their parents and leave for the US will find themselves far from home (though only 90 miles away, it seems even farther when you can't go back). They will work harder than they ever imagined and they will long for the social connections that Cuba provides. If they are fortunate they will have the clothing and cars, the bright lights, but will feel an emptiness that only Cuba can fill. At the end of it all, they too will become true believers in something more meaningful and more valuable than the material.

WHEN FIDEL DIES

It is sheer folly to assume that the Revolution will die with Fidel, although rumors abound about his successor; Raul, the feared younger brother of Fidel, is mentioned, as is some young doctor who is being groomed to step into the *Comandante's* shoes. If Fidel remains as healthy and as lucky as he has been in the past - 637 assassination attempts by the CIA with no luck—then he will probably live long enough for Elián, the national hero, to grow up, mature, get a good Cuban education and take over the reins of the socialist nation. Most Cubans residing in Cuba will tell you that yes, the *Comandante*/ the "bearded one"/ *papa* directs the country's socialist mechanisms. The essence of socialism, however, lies deep in the hearts and midst of its people.

A majority of Cubans feel that life since the Revolution is infinitely better than it was before, and they would rather die than give up the gains they have made as a country. Thoughts about life in Cuba after the death of Fidel range from feelings of resignation, "I will leave when he dies, I won't want to live in Cuba," stated by a young Cuban male, to "I am fearful of what will happen to my country," expressed by an older woman. The one thing most Cubans seem to be certain of however, is that they will not lie down and concede their country to some outside entity. "We are ready for any attack, we have been preparing for 45 years," confidently declares a young woman who is a museum guide. More strongly expressed was the view of a middle-aged college professor: "The only way that Cuba will be defeated is to drive us into the sea."

Whether the government has managed to bring the socialist dream into full fruition may be questionable to some Cubans, especially the old-timers who have been most invested in the success of the Revolution. What a majority of Cuban people do not doubt, however, is that the lives of most Cubans have improved in the 45 years after the Revolution. Feelings remain strong against a possible attack or takeover of their country by a foreign power. "Blood will run in the streets," says an old man who remembers life in Cuba before the Revolution. "We will not go back to that," referring to the wretched life of most black and rural Cubans who lived as peasants before the Revolution. As essential

47

as literacy, good healthcare, and adequate housing, what the Revolution brought them was dignity.

The Revolution gave the nation dignity by requiring everyone at some juncture to do the work, as well as educating and eliminating the peasant class. The old-line plantation owners who expect to come back and claim their estates in Cuba will be hard-pressed, for they will find their peasant labor force among the literate Cuban population. They will be less able to establish a working poor like those who labor in the sweatshops of other South American and Asian countries.

I asked a Cuban friend if there really was popular support for Fidel. He said that "there are four types of Cubans: one-fourth are true *Fidelistas*; one-fourth are true Marxists; one-fourth are in the Black Market and they don't care who is in power or what type of government we have; and one-fourth hate Fidel and socialism. Now you figure out why Fidel is still in power if three-quarters of the people are for the government that we have." I told this story to another Cuban friend who replied that the breakdown was incorrect. She stated that there are only two kinds of Cubans: one-half are *Fidelistas* and the other half, Marxists; and anyone, because of the economic blockade, would use the Black Market if they had to. It appears that the majority of Cubans are satisfied with Fidel and the form of government that they have. This might explain why, after almost 45 years, Fidel has yet to be deposed.

It seems that with or without the leadership of Fidel, the Cuban people believe in their sovereignty and their right to be self-determining. What is apparent is that Cuba will never again be what she was, and the belief that Cubans will return to those "good old days" is delusional at best. Cuba is who she is; she has found herself, and like any self-actualized entity, she cannot go back to being the way she was. As bad as things may be now, she maintains herself and refuses to be anything else.

CULTURE VERSUS IDEOLOGY

Before Cuba was communist, socialist, or any other political label that one may wish to ascribe it, Cuba was collectivistic. Collectivism characterizes 70% of the world's population; its members are integrated into strong cohesive groups that stress a "we" consciousness, of interdependence, cooperation, sharing of resources, social welfare. Cubans are bound together by a value system that celebrates family, responsibility, and collective spirituality. This cultural tradition has enabled the vast majority to survive enslavement, oppression, exploitation, and now the particular hardships faced during the Special Period.

Prior to the Revolution, individualistic values were the political, social, and economic norm in Cuba. The "I" consciousness and principles of individual initiative, competition, and exploitation dominated Cuban society, allowing for a small group of privileged Cubans to accumulate wealth and enjoy the "good life" as the labor of black Cubans was exploited.

Collectivity was the foundation of a consciousness that enabled blacks, mulattos, and poor white Cubans to survive a pre-Revolutionary Cuban society. Families shared, nurtured, and cared for each other. Reciprocity between individuals and groups and responsibility to the community was the norm, demonstrating that one family's good fortune benefited family and friends alike. Life was miserable for most in pre-revolutionary Cuba, but was made bearable because of the sense of connectedness and communalism that prevailed. These pre-revolutionary values endured and continue to shape the lives of Cubans today.

Obtaining food and necessities has become a trial of daily life since the Special Period. Cubans will tell you that, for a while, life was good. The problems began however, with the collapse of the Soviet Union. Between 1989 and 1992, a heavily dependent Cuba lost seventy percent of its trade. In 1991 Fidel declared "a Special Period in the time of peace" as a direct result of the US embargo. The Special Period has persisted now for over ten years. Cubans were confronted with acute food shortages, malnutrition-related diseases, the absence of medicine, a lack of gasoline, and the loss of products such as soap and toothpaste for personal hygiene.

Perhaps the greatest achievement of the Cuban people has been their ability to remain true to their cultural essence in a time of great hardship. Their cultural core is rooted in collectivism, they have not wavered in the face of extreme deprivation. *No es fácil* is repeated like a mantra in Cuba today, and life continues to be a constant challenge.

Despite extreme adversity, the Cuban people have not succumbed to the attitude of individualism that is so often produced by poverty. Cubans have endured the kinds of deprivation that would have destroyed most societies. But the country has held together. Her people surprisingly have not developed consciousness of lack, nor have they succumbed to the selfishness of looking out for number one. Deep-seated and pervasive free-floating anger is not evident in the majority of Cubans. Crime and exploitation are not rampant. In some sense, this cultural core of the Cuban people has made them stronger and more determined.

Cubans are collectivistic, communal people. Individualism is not a Cuban cultural value. If imposed, Cubans will revolt against it as they did in 1959. Cubans have used collectivistic values to survive, and are now utilizing these same values to thrive. Collectivistic values have enabled Cuba, despite almost insurmountable odds, to far out-distance her neighbors in terms of providing food, shelter, health care and education to all of its populace. In forty short years, Cuba has made strides that few industrialized nations can even boast.

MY WAY: THE INSATIABLE DESIRE TO BE SELF-DETERMINING

Some Cubans alive today have known nothing but the US blockade against their country, yet for over 35 years, Cuba has persevered in the struggle to go its own way. The heads of Cubans may be bloodied from the almost forty-five year blockade and embargo, but they remain unbowed. Against the United States, Cubans liken themselves to the heroic David confronted by the powerful Goliath. Defiantly, they vow never to submit. Cubans continue to fight for their right as a nation to act as a sovereign power and to shape their own future. They have a notion—an idea of who they believe they are, who they want to be, and will resist any outside influence to change this view of themselves.

One day, history will absolve Cuba. The now considered rebellious youth will be respected as the wise old woman, the one who knew all the while who she was, that she was different, and most importantly, that she would not be molded into something that simply is not her. Cuba is a beacon for the future with universal education, health care and adequate housing for her entire people. These are rights that the world over need, desire, and deserve.

No matter what comes, Cuba is determined to be a socialist island in the sea of capitalism. The last forty-five years since the Revolution has been the first time in their history that Cubans have been self-determining. They are bent on cutting their unique path through history and walking to the beat of a different drum, establishing an economic, political, and social system that they consider best for their country. They are serious when they preach it and do not take lightly the vow painted on walls: *Socialismo o muerto,* Socialism or death.

While the fall of the Soviet Union had a tremendous and disastrous economic impact on the country, Cubans have came to know their strength and resolve as a nation. They have grown into themselves, alas: alone, isolated, ostracized and punished for the world, they held their heads high and proclaimed that to be Cuban is to be self-determining.

Cuba is the unquenchable desire to be autonomous and self-determining. The National Anthem would do well to be "My Way," as they are determined to be who they are despite the odds. Their resolve is not tempered by sanctions, and in the face of imposed restrictions they proudly protest their capacity to remain unbound.

The national bird is the Cuban Trogon. Adorned in blue, white, and red plume, it mirrors the colors of the flag. The bird is a symbol of freedom. It seems a fitting representation of the spirit of the Cuban people, for the bird dies when kept in captivity. Cuba, like the bird, will no longer exist if it succumbs to the whims of the powerful, if it is forced into submission. An old man repeated to me the words of José Martí: "Hunger is temporary, but if you lose your dignity, the effects last forever." If its people give up their dignity, their passion to be self-determining, then Cuba will no longer exist. Under United States' or any other control, the land mass known as Cuba will cease to be.

A WAY OUT OF NO WAY

When I visit Cuba, I experience a strange sort of familiarity. I am reminded of my days growing up in the US South during the 1950s. Life was extremely hard for southern blacks then, but they possessed strength of spirit that enabled them to transcend the adversity that they faced. I recognize this same spirit in the Cuban people. Rather than breaking them, the US embargo and the Special Period that followed has made them stronger. Like empowered Blacks in the US, they have searched deep within themselves, tapping into a reservoir of strength, persistence, and ingenuity that has enabled them to reclaim their nation. Like their cousins whose ancestors were delivered on slave ships to Charleston and Annapolis, these descendants of the enslaved have learned to make a way out of no way.

I was always amazed at how blacks in the US, especially in the rural south, were able to make a life despite dire circumstances. Feeding a family was difficult at best for many Blacks in the rural south. They hunted, fished, and supplemented their meager diets with small family gardens. From the days of slavery, Blacks had learned how to take the most undesirable parts of the pig such as the intestines and the feet, and turn them into culinary delicacies. I have seen them make a "home" in a shotgun house with wooden windows, door hinges made of discarded leather straps, and old newspaper tacked on walls to guard against the bitter winter cold; children huddled together under quilts made of scraps of old worn clothes. Today, these pieces of cloth sewn together by countless grandmothers for strictly utilitarian uses are considered works of art and hang in museums in the US.

During the 1950s many southern Blacks either could not afford the money necessary to visit a doctor or were refused treatment by the white doctors in the area. As a result, they reached back into their cultural roots and utilized the medicinal herbs that were available. Folk remedies healed and kept many a Black child healthy during those days. When the Soviets left Cuba, they took with them a steady supply of modern antibiotics. Cubans had to use their resourcefulness to discover alternative treatments. As a result, when one visits a local Cuban pharmacy, one will also see a variety of homeopathic remedies, and natural tincture.

Cubans have used the same sense of resourcefulness especially with their cars. Deprived of new parts since the end of Soviet aid, Cuban farmers now use oxen to replace Soviet-era tractors, and ingenious Cubans keep 1950s-era cars running by turning a junked piece of metal into a gasket or cylinder.

Fighting starvation became a priority for Cubans during the Special Period. While southern Blacks used burned corn meal to simulate coffee grinds, Cubans made burgers out of grapefruit and orange peels. Cuba has today made a remarkable recovery from the food crisis brought on by the collapse of trade relations with the former Soviet Bloc and the tightening of the US trade embargo. Unable to import food and materials needed for conventional agriculture, Cuba turned inward for self-reliance. The struggle to provide food for the populace has spawned far-reaching innovations, and human ingenuity has significantly transformed food production.

Organic farming took root in Cuba because of the shortage of chemical pesticides, herbicides and gas-fueled machines. As a result of their resourcefulness during these hard times, Cuba leads the world sustainable agriculture, organic farming, animal traction, biological pest control, and waste minimization. Today Cuba is the world leader in the field of organic agriculture.

A remarkable consequence of Cuba's food shortage has been the creation of urban gardens. Frustrated by deepening food shortages, Cubans decided to take matters into their own hands and started growing their own food, even in urban areas like Havana. They sowed seeds in backyards, on rooftops, neighborhood lots, and even baseball fields. There are now over 30,000 private gardens in Havana that produce traditional crops like yucca, taro, onions, and cilantro and provide thirty percent of the food supply. Amazing also, schools, hospitals, and even businesses have created gardens to supply their cafeterias and kitchens. Many urban gardeners grow their own medicinal herbs. It is a beautiful sight to see while walking down wide avenues and crowded streets in Havana.

Because of the loss of Soviet trade and the US embargo Cubans had to learn to be creative with what they had. When asked how they make do, Cubans will often say *inventamos*, "we invent." Through this period of adversity, their unique brand of resourcefulness has enabled Cubans to resist against all odds. Cubans have discovered what they are made of, who they really are. If and when the political and economic climate changes, the challenge that lies ahead will attest to whether or not they can sustain a uniquely Cuban identity. For now I am comfortable knowing that I can still feel at home in Cuba and even enjoy some healthy, organically grown food.

AFRICA REBORN IN THE WESTERN HEMISPHERE

A twenty-seven year old *babalawo* (father of secrets) recites the language and practices the rites of Ifá, the 8,000 year-old African spiritual system practiced by the Yoruba. If material things are a sign of the good life, *Santería,* or Ifá adherents in destitute Havana enjoy small luxuries such as bathrooms, automatic washers, cell phones, jewelry, and the ubiquitous gold teeth. In Cuba, the religion thrives as young people increasingly see evidence that *Santería* provides them the power to improve their lives.

Santería is a syncretism, a blend of both the ancient African monotheistic[1] religion of the Yoruba people, who were brought from Nigeria to the New World as slaves, and the Catholicism practiced by their captors. Yoruba brought to Cuba were forbidden to practice their religion by Spanish enslavers, and in order to safely continue their spiritual traditions, the enslaved Africans identified and disguised their deities with some of the Catholic saints worshipped by the Spaniards. In this way, the enslaved were able to venerate their deities without the danger of punishment. The spiritual philosophy stayed intact while the outward expressions became masked in the symbols of Catholicism.

1.	Those who are ignorant of African spiritual philosophies or have used these misnomers to justify slavery and colonization often chide African religions as "polytheistic". There are no African polytheistic religions. Ancient Africans were well aware that a created being cannot fully contemplate its Creator; this would be like a single grain of sand trying to contemplate a beach or a single fish trying to understand the vast expanse of the oceans. Instead, the Source is acknowledged for being the wellspring of all potentialities of creation and manifestation, and that daily spiritual practice deals with specializing in aspects of this Divine whole that can be contemplated, and through these aspects, experience a connection to the totality of the Divine Consciousness. These ancient African Mystery Systems heavily contributed to the base of spiritual/philosophical concepts such as the I am, The Omniscience, Omnipresence, Omnipotence, and Ultimate Singularity of the Creator; the Tree of Life and Spiritual Psychology; Divine Law (Order); The Power of Belief; Transcendental Meditation; and It - The Unchanging Being that is both the No-thing, the Source of All Potentialities, and All-Things, the Totality of Manifested Creation, The Oneness of All Creation, found in the major religions of today.

Keeping the Yoruba religion alive was an act of resistance that demonstrated the refusal of the enslaved to submit to both the ideologies of slavery and white supremacy. It was faith in African deities that gave the enslaved Africans strength to endure and protest the brutality of slavery. Despite being raped, brutalized and worked to death, Africans built a spiritual oasis in the New World. The *santeros*, or practitioners of *Santería*, used the symbols of the oppressor's religion to maintain their African power. *Santería* is a testament to the strength of the human spirit in the midst of unbearable suffering.

It appears that Cubans cannot and will not be separated from their cultural center. This tenacity was evident during the years of strict Marxism. The practice of Ifá, the African spiritual system that forms the spiritual foundation of *Santería*, survived despite then being outlawed by the state. Today *Santería* is more vibrant than ever.

Everywhere in Cuba there is evidence of the *Santería* religion. From initiates dressed in the traditional white clothing to the man or woman wearing the brightly colored red and white or green and yellow beads, the religion is ubiquitous. *Santería* attracts practitioners from all walks of life, from the college professor to the taxi driver. While it is traditionally an African religion, Cubans of all hues, whether white, mulatto, or black, practice it.

The influence is pervasive. To my surprise, the taxi driver that took us to an address where a *Santería* ceremony was being held showed up later as a *babalawo* and participated in the ceremony. When we tried to locate friends of ours in Centro Habana, home to most *Santeros*, we were surprised and delighted to hear that they had traded houses with another family (houses are not privately owned) for religious purposes. It seems that our friend who is himself a *babalawo*, wanted to conduct sacrifices more efficiently. He lived in a second-story apartment before, and now proudly shows his new apartment complete with a tile at the entrance honoring his guiding saint.

Santeros will proudly tell you that Fidel is a believer. It is said that African spirits protect him, and that this connection to God is what keeps him safe. His mother is said to have offered flowers to the Patron

Saint of Cuba, *La Virgen del Cobre*, when Fidel and Raul were fighting in the mountains. According to the stories, he has had lions sacrificed for him in Africa. It is even reported that a local *Santera* watches over Fidel.

One of my most memorable experiences was having a meal of stewed goat, black beans, and rice with seven *babalawos*. Seated at the table was an esteemed *padrino*, three middle-aged *babalawos* and three *babalawos* in their twenties. The conversation was quite interesting. They discussed the relationship between the Yoruba religion and ancient Egypt [Ifá being an unbroken extension of the African mystery systems (schools) that originated in Ethiopia, spread through Nubia to Egypt, and migrated back down throughout the continent after Egypt fell to foreign invaders]; their disappointment that more Africans do not practice their own religion instead of Islam and Christianity, especially since the roots of both are in Ethiopia and Egypt, drawing from the same spiritual wellspring that Ifá drew from and contributed to many millennia ago. They discussed the importance of being connected to one's culture.

The concern of the *babalawos* is understood when you consider that it is often argued by Cubans and some Africans that traditional African culture has been better preserved and is thus more intact in Cuba than anywhere else in the world, including some parts of Africa, and Brazil. Cuba is where the sixteenth-century language of the Yoruba religion has been preserved. While the Yoruba religion began in the Nigerian city of Ilé-Ifè, it is to Cuba that even Nigerian *babalawos* come to study the classical language of the religion. *Ñáñigos*, African social or national groups that no longer exist in Africa are said to survive in Cuba. Everywhere, in the faces of the people, the air, the music, the dance, and most of all the practice of the ancient Yoruba religion, born in the New World as *Santería*, Africa lives. To be Cuban is to be touched in some way by Africa.

ENERGY DOES NOT LIE

Those who have traveled to Cuba speak of the incredible energy that seems to pulse through every aspect of Cuban life. This energy invades your senses as soon as you land at José Martí Airport, and only grows in intensity, as you increasingly become a part of Cuba. At times, the visit to Cuba can feel almost overwhelming as you are swept up in this energy. You experience this in the people, the colors, the flora, the music, the Malecon. It flows from children in the streets, old men playing checkers, women chatting from their balconies.

There is actually a higher, faster, vibrating field of energy in Cuba. Students of quantum physics and human energy will say that this feeling is real and that there is a plausible reason for its existence. The universe is composed of bands of vibrating energy, and this includes human beings, as we are composed of concentrated energy fields. Our emotions and attitudes emit energy fields that vibrate at different frequencies. These energy fields can be calibrated and to measure the energy of human consciousness.

A culture's energy is an expression of its awareness, and some societies calibrate at slower levels while the energy of others calibrate at much faster frequencies. Economic development does not necessarily correlate with higher levels of consciousness. The force released by consumer societies and collective societies are immensely different. Consumerism is known to produce states of consciousness that vibrate at slower, more dangerous frequencies. Living in a consumer society is destructive to those unable to be good consumers, as one's esteem and value as a human being is determined by their ability to accumulate wealth and possessions.

Researchers like Dr. David Hawkins have quantified the levels of human consciousness. Hawkins has found that low vibrating energy is destructive to both individuals and to societies at large, while faster vibrating energies are constructive expressions of power. According to him, aspects of human consciousness—such as shame, apathy, fear and anger—vibrate at slow frequencies. Courage is described as a frequency at which power first appears; it is a critical line that distinguishes the positive and negative influences of life.

The shame experienced in consumer societies produces either a suicide of the spirit—depression, substance abuse, criminal behavior or actual taking of life—as has occurred in the United States during the Great Depression of the 1930s. Shame vibrates at the lowest level of consciousness and is compared to death. It is a major emotion resulting from "consumer failure." Feelings of shame lead to vulnerability to other slow vibrating energies such as apathy, fear, and desire. These negative emotions often lead to addiction, greed, and anger, which generate crime and violence in consumer societies.

The slower vibrating energy associated with the fear of not being able to consume, the insatiable craving for "things," and the frustration, stress, anxiety and free-floating anger that is present in consumer societies cannot be found in any large measure in Cuba. The energy that a traveler to Cuba experiences is noticeably different from what one might feel in a consumer society. Despite the many hardships endured by the Cuban people during the Special Period, their energy is unlike that found in the urban ghettos of the United States. The lowest level of consciousness, shame, appears to be absent among Cuban people, because the sense of being a non-person does not appear to exist.

While the Cuban people may have less, and may even be considered to be poor by some standards, they do not live in the slow energy state of apathy produced by shame and characterized by despair and hopelessness. The resourcefulness and ingenuity of the Cuban people creates a faster vibrating energy that makes apathy impossible.

Interestingly, it is those aspects of consciousness possessed by the Cuban people that vibrate at higher, faster frequencies. The energy that is so pervasive in Cuba decries what most of us have read or heard about the misery of Cuban people. Foremost, the energy possessed by and exuded by the Cuban people is a reflection of a higher level of human consciousness and expression of their power.

What the traveler to Cuba finds most comforting is the absence of the energy of fear of crime and violence that the consumer consciousness creates. Courage, the ability to deal with life challenges and the gateway to higher, faster vibrating energies is the consciousness that best describes the Cuban people. At this level of consciousness, obstacles become stimulants and power first appears. True power is demonstrated as the people are no longer willing to be the pawns of any other nation and exert their right to autonomy. This consciousness is also the "zone" of exploration, accomplishment, fortitude, and determination, all characteristics of the Cuban people. Apathy is a state of helplessness; its victims lack not only resources, but also the energy to avail themselves to what is available.

The cornerstone of Cuban society is the concept of the "New Man and New Woman" who use their individual talents to elevate the whole of society. Through their indomitable commitment to service, Cubans give back to the society, as much energy as they take. In return, they receive energy that is self-reinforcing: positive feedback, intrinsic reward, high self-esteem and an extraordinary pride in their country.

Cuba is alive with a higher, faster energy that prospers and protects its people against all negative outside forces that wish to destroy it. The energy that the traveler to Cuba feels is real; it is the energy that empowers the Cuban people.

HOW DEEP IS YOUR LOVE

We were on a tour of Santiago de Cuba, making our way to the tomb of Cuba's national hero, José Martí. As we drove up to the memorial we passed an enormous monument of large black machetes, on our right side, breaking out of the ground and pointing at the sky. To the immediate left there stood a giant statue of a man riding gallantly on a horse. It was of Antonio Maceo, the Black General that was destined to be President of the new, Independent Cuba. Over the tomb hung a gigantic Cuban flag, and guarding the Tomb of José Martí were three black male soldiers.

At the monument, we were told that a change of the guard occurred every half hour, and it happened that we arrived shortly before the 30-minute mark. At the onset of this ceremony, loud drumming music began from the sentry's quarters and out came three black soldiers (a sister in the middle and two brothers on the flanks) marching in a Cuban style goose-step to the rhythm of the beat. The goose-step was not the standard "up-down" goose-step. In the Cuban goose-step the soldiers' leg would hang in the sky for a long while, then drop to the ground, while the next one stood in the sky for another long while, and this was repeated again and again in rhythm until arrival at the tomb. Each soldier was also carrying a rifle on one arm, maintaining a balance so perfect that it seemed almost impossible.

Out from nowhere, the song "How Deep is Your Love" came into my head, and I began to hum it as tears rolled down my face. I had not heard this tune in at least 20 years. It was then that I realized what the Cuban Revolution of 1959 stood for: it was a conclusion to the slave rebellion against the Spanish that would have granted Cuban independence by 1898. That hope for independence was dashed when Cuba was again occupied by the US after Spanish defeat. It was not until much later, in 1959, that the delayed dream of José Martí, Antonio Maceo and the Cuban people came true. Independence, at last.

This is why the three monuments are placed together in the heart of Santiago de Cuba. It was from the slave rebellions that Spanish rule saw its last days over Cuban soil; it was from the leadership of

Maceo that the masses could rise in liberation from their Colonial master; and it was from the inspiration of Martí's speeches and writings that the aspirations for freedom in the hearts of the Cuban people could be articulated and directed into positive action.

Many people have formed opinions about the Cuban Revolution within the limited construct of the Cold War. This perspective lacks a true sense of history, knowledge, and context from which the Cuban Revolution arose. The Cuban Revolution is often erroneously perceived as a rebellion against the tyranny of the Batista regime, but it was actually the continuation of a rebellion against foreign rule and oppression.

The Cuban Revolution of 1959 was the Haitian Revolution that worked. After Haiti, Cuba was the second Black[2] country in the Western Hemisphere to achieve total independence from its colonial masters. It was not the political independence "awarded" to colonies worldwide in the 1960s, 70s, and 80s. Unfortunately, Haiti had a blockade placed upon it by the West that has existed since the 1830s for its crime of rebelling against its colonial master. Cuba had a blessing in the military strength of the Soviets that protected her against immediate recolonization. This relationship was later soured by the hierarchies of 'developed' and 'developing,' of North and South that existed in Cuba's association with the Soviet Union. Cuba went through the pain of separation from the Soviets during the Special Period, and although life is still hard because of the Blockade, self-determination is a reality being actualized in the hearts, minds, and bodies of Cuban people living on their own terms.

---

2.   Cuba was more clearly described by Cubans after the Revolution as being a 'Latin-African' country, something that, if stated in the past, would have been paramount to blasphemy.

BATÁ

In "post-modern" Cuba, time does not exist. What was, is. What is, always was. According to Ifá, *Orishas* are manifestations of the individual, collective, and nature consciousness. They serve as sources of guidance and strength – deriving their power from the human will, and more specifically from the Source, the Creator.

The Creator grants the use of ashé (asé), the enabling force, to humans to perform acts of co-creation and self-realization according to Its Will. At every public performance that is attended in today's Cuba, the *Orishas* are invoked and acknowledged through the playing of batá drums and through ritualized dancers representing an archetype within the human psyche that is reflected out into the physical world. From ballet to big-band concerts, from hip-hop clubs to the *Tropicana*, the bateros will play and the *Orisha* will dance. The drum and the *Orishas* will always be the heart of Cuba.

TRULY ORGANIC

For those in search of "organic" food, go no further than to Cuba. The Special Period combined with the US blockade, left Cubans without the financial resources that would have enabled them to purchase agrichemicals and petroleum for farming in "conventional," hi-tech agriculture.

Farmers were brought to the table to sit as equals with scientists and work out the best course of development for Cuban agriculture. The farmers were asked, "What worked in the past?" Scientists were asked, "How can you improve on this traditional (sustainable) knowledge?"

Scientists intensified the traditional knowledge held by farmers. They included growing predators of plant parasites and pathogens in order to more effectively regulate pathogenic threats to the plants, creating systems of plant rotations to control weed species, encouraging the growing of legumes as a protein food source and a means of mitigating soil salinization, and converting organic waste into energy, food for livestock, and fertilizer.

Farmers talked of using insects to feed on the insects that plagued the plants that grew and of the benefits that came with planting two types of crops in the same field (one above-ground crop, one below-ground crop) in order to deny weeds space to grow - methods considered primitive and impossible in "conventional" monocrop export agriculture. In using traditional methods such as these, the need for pesticides and herbicides were negated. These were organic solutions to questions in "modern" agriculture.

By using a system of revolving bovine grazing, cows are moved onto the last season's fields in order to fertilize them, and alternated when it is time to plant on each field, giving nutrients back to the soil during dormant periods and moving them onto newly harvested fields in order to restore them. Farmers also use oxen with special plows that cut under the surface of soil in order to enrich the soil to prevent erosion. Methods such as these eliminate the need for fertilizer.

Juaquin Santiago

Probably the most important aspect of "organic" agriculture is in giving farmers the proper respect that they deserve as contributors to the total health of a people. When they are disparaged, the quality of the food that we consume is disparaged. When profit and productivity become more important than balance, equal productivity decreases as well as the nutritious value of food, and food safety.

The state of mind that Cuba represents is one of life - a sustainable and purposeful life. The new society of post-revolution Cuba is one of self-actualization and the appreciation of the gifts of others, because gifts that are contributed to the community pot help society thrive, and sustain life in its full vibrancy.

THE RHYTHM IN MY BLOOD

When someone mentions Cuba, the first thing that comes to mind is the island air, thick and humid, punctuated by waves crashing against the Malecon, the river wall. Then I hear salsa music and rumbas, son and guanguanco. Latin rhythm, gyrations and sensual playfulness, accentuated by an African heartbeat. I remember smiles in every skin color, excited generosity, genuine hospitality. I recall the image of classic cars broken down on the side of the road, driving past those that have miraculously been brought back to life.

Cuba is not just a place, it is a feeling. It is the sense of humanity that exists in each of us. It's that euphoric unknown that makes people smile unabashedly or sigh with satisfaction. It is the spirit of revolutionaries united in the struggle.

Prior to arriving in Cuba, my first thoughts were those of fear. As I was escorted off the plane and lined up at the customs office, a plain white wall stood between me and the unknown. Small hallways led to windows where each person was individually questioned. I stood in line, not sure of my fate. I recalled popular images in the media, of tyrannical dictators and helpless citizens being carted off to face unknown doom. I remembered everyone who warned me against traveling to Cuba and I thought about the movies that I had seen where people went on vacation only to end up in some far away jail for a crime they never committed. I took a deep breath and hoped for the best. Needless to say, I was easily granted admission and the quiet of the customs checkpoint broke into the chaos of a metropolitan airport. I was expertly moved through the bustle with the help of a Cuban travel agent and I made it to my hotel without delay.

That night I slept off the jetlag, and when the sun dawned on my first Cuban morning I learned what it really meant to be in Cuba. I left the hotel to explore Havana Vieja (Old Havana). There was such poverty, yet unexpected smiles and playful laughter lurked around every corner. The buildings were old and falling apart. Several empty lots evidenced the remains of structures that could no longer bear to continue standing. The people walked around in clothes that had long lost the look of newness. School-aged children wore uniforms. The more I looked, the more I noticed that although clothes were old, they were clean and pressed. Everyone seemed to have their hair done and the men were neatly shaven.

There was a dignity to these people. They were not victims of poverty; their spirits rose above it. I began to see past the crumbling buildings, with chipped, faded paint and layers of dust. I began to look past the barefoot children with recycled clothes in muted colors. I started to see a people filled with dignity, making the best of what they had. Strangers greeted me as I walked along. The innocence and exuberance of youth was embodied by all generations. Card tables were set up in the street near open doors. Children sat on front stoops and friends gathered to play dominoes and share stories. Neighbors greeted each other from open windows, and soccer balls skirted along the roads with jubilant children in excited pursuit. It was a place that made me smile.

When I was first confronted with the poverty, it was distressing. But then I saw that these people were living, that they were enjoying each other. They were experiencing the humanity that comes from solidarity. This was a true community where everyone belonged. Walking through the streets of Vedado and Havana Vieja I knew that I was not Cuban, but I saw something in Cubans that I saw in myself. I witnessed a joy that I had not experienced in years and a freedom of spirit that inspires me even today.

Prior to this trip, I had not encountered a large Cuban population. I know a few Cubans but they all have Spanish characteristics, fair skin and light colored hair and eyes. On the island, Cubans came in a variety of skin shades, from the deepest ebony to the creamiest alabaster, but everyone I met with told me how they were linked to Africa. There is pride in their African blood, an understanding of their culture. It's a Cuba that most tourists miss out on. It's a country full of pride and sprit and understanding of self.

With my tour book in one hand and a digital camera in the other, I set out to explore in depth the area of Havana known as Vedado. I stopped to take pictures of the landmarks the publisher said were noteworthy. While distracted by the majestic simplicity of the architecture, a Cuban with a charcoal complexion approached me. He blurted out a few words in a colloquial Cuban dialect with which I was unfamiliar. When I didn't respond right away he said in traditional Spanish, " I thought you were Cuban." His name was Oscar and he then proceeded to give me a behind the scenes tour of the city. I saw where the Cubans live and how they spend their days.

Oscar told me what his everyday life was like. He asked lots of questions about the US. Oscar was a few years younger than me, but we had a lot in common. I was surprised by his knowledge of current events in the United States, especially since the American government keeps its citizens ignorant of Cuban affairs.

We walked past a group of teenagers playing street ball (basketball), in a rundown court at a forlorn park. The scene could have been in any inner-city basketball court in the US and a wave of cultural displacement disoriented me. The parallel was dizzying; I forgot that I was in a foreign land. When I snapped out of it, Oscar was talking about his favorite NBA stars and I began to feel ashamed of our wealth as Americans.

After walking for some time in the oppressive Caribbean humidity, Oscar asked if I had ever had a *guarapo*. Made from pressed sugar cane, it is a juice that is said to rejuvenate. I confessed that I hadn't, so Oscar took me to an apartment building off a main street in Vedado. He yelled to the people upstairs and they invited us up. I got very excited because Oscar said that a famous Cuban singer owned this apartment. The makeshift restaurant was on the second floor and to get there I climbed the narrowest walled-in staircase in my life. There were people watching television in the living room. They greeted us and didn't seem surprised to have strangers in their home.

Oscar led us out onto the balcony where there were modest tables set up and some European tourists elbow-deep in plates of lobster. A young caramel colored Cuban woman came to ask what we wanted and Oscar ordered us each a *guarapo*. Sitting in the comfort of this private home Oscar and the other makeshift tour guides, who lured tourists to restaurants and cafés for a free meal and small commission, began to open up about their lives in Cuba. One Cuban man with skin tinted like mahogany, revealed that he had been for the revolution and that Cuba was supposed to be free but now he didn't feel free. The embargo, more precisely stated as the Blockade of Cuba by the US, keeps Cuba and Cubans in a state of distress. Supplying Cuba with medicines and foodstuffs is grounds for very tangible threats of sanctions by the US.

He talked about how he had fought in Angola because it was his duty as an African. I asked him how long he had lived in Cuba. He smiled at me and said since his family was brought here. He reached across the table and touched my arm and said, "I'm African, you are African, and Cuba is African." In one simple gesture, a man that I had just met changed my life.

I was raised as an African American. I was a black individual in my country. I had to get mine as everyone else was getting theirs; I wasn't part of anything bigger. Yes, I belonged to my parents, my church, my school or my neighborhood, but anything outside was unfamiliar and therefore hostile. I lived in an "us" versus "them" world: they didn't know us and we didn't know them. But when this stranger touched my brown skin, his words connected me to who I am. I looked in this man's eyes and I saw my grandfather, my great grandfather, my uncles and cousins. We were connected; I was part of something universal. With one look this man saw the Africa in me and it was a source of pride for both of us.

The next day a copper-beige man asked me why my Spanish sounded funny. His name was Alfredo and his son, a world-class gymnast, recently defected to the United States. We talked about his worry for his son. He asked me about the violence in movies that were set in US cities and how realistic or fictionalized it was. We talked about education and other opportunities in our respective countries. He was worried about his son and it showed in his sad eyes and distracted reflections. He asked me when my parents left Cuba. I tried to explain that I was the descendant of African slaves brought to the United States. He gave me one look and dismissed my explanation. He shook his head and said you're in Cuba, so you are Cuban. I have never been in a culture that, with one glance can be so accepting of others.

I was recruited to translate for some friends when I experienced a spiritual reading in the tradition of *Santería*. I sat in a small apartment and witnessed spiritual prophecy and the reenactment of African traditions dating back to when the first Africans were brought to the island. I heard them playing drums, felt the drums in my heartbeat. I heard them chant, heard the chants in my breathing. I saw them move and dance and felt the rhythms of dances long forgotten in my bones. I saw the Cuban youths transformed into African holy men. I heard them speaking ancient Yoruba and although I didn't understand the words, I understood the sentiment. They were the roots of the gospel music that I had sung as a child.

When I returned the next day to the apartment, I was treated more like a relative than a guest. The door was swung open and everyone greeted me as if I was a frequent visitor. The function of the household reminded me of my home when my great grandmother was alive. It was the model of a traditional African American household. The clear matriarch welcomed everyone and ran the home with the love, confidence, and command that can only be found in a "big mama."

I found myself participating in this house as I would in my own. I was soon answering the door and fetching things from other parts of the house for this embodiment of my lost matriarch. They treated me like I was at home and I felt like it. Here in Cuba I found people, black people, who acted and responded to life in the same way as my family. It was the physical personification of a once lost tradition. They were speaking a different language, but somehow they were my family. I left for the US later that week and the women of the house cried for me like I would never return. They kissed my face and wished me a safe voyage as if I was their only son leaving home for the first time.

"It's in your blood," someone told me in a nightclub one night as I struggled to learn Salsa. "Black people are the same everywhere" was what another Cuban said after my friend got up and started dancing spontaneously to a far-off rhythm. Many times people in the United

States claim to be just American. Children are taught to fill out paperwork with "Other" or "American." We have rejected any idea of distinctiveness. We embrace a generic American culture where no one belongs and everyone strives to fit into some impossible ideal presented by the media.

Cuba is many things. It is Latin and African, Poor yet proud, revolutionary yet welcoming and understanding. I went to Cuba to learn about their education and was in turn educated about myself. Cuba is time warp where you are forced to see your past, your history, and your true nature. Cuba is a mirror that reflects not the physical, but the actual. You are forced to answer for your privilege and wealth, time and education. Cuba is a place where people celebrate their similarities and their differences. It took a trip to Cuba to remember the Africa that had been repressed by slavery and oppression. I love Cuba, for its beauty, for its women, for its humanity, and for the culture that accepts my funny Spanish and bad Salsa, and sees in me someone who is just like them.

About the Travelers

The three travelers that contributed to this book are travelers who experience and write about the human consciousness of the places that they travel to. They look to document the cultural, political, economic, and environmental consciousness of the locales that they visit.

The Spiritual Traveler moves on next to Micronesia, and then on the New Orleans.

Join us in experiencing Volumes II and III of the Spiritual Traveler, *Micronesia: The Good Life* and *New Orleans: The Essence of the Big Easy.*

Other titles in the *The Spiritual Traveler Series*
by blue ocean press coming out in 2007

The Spiritual Traveler Series provides the reader with a new type of travel writing experience. Instead of simply looking at the sights, sounds, and tastes of a locale, the Spiritual Traveler allows the reader to experience the consciousness of a nation.

"The tourist takes in the sights; the traveler sees the reality of the landscape."

The Spiritual Traveler Vol. II
Micronesia: The Good Life
p.w. long
ISBN: 978-4-902837-02-1

What is the "good life"? Is it a given or must we earn it? Must we give up something to get it? On her trip to Micronesia, Majuro (the Marshall Islands), Pohnpei, and Chuuk, the traveler pondered the meaning of the "good life". What better place on earth to consider this question than the these islands so bountifully blessed by nature. Upon reaching the Marshall Islands, the Pearl of the Pacific, the traveler is sure that on these islands, indeed the true good life is experienced. She is saddened however, to learn that many of the Marshallese have forsaken that life for a few deadly baubles; white sugar, flour, salt, and rice. The traveler experiences the incredible beauty of Pohnpei, the mysteries of Nan Madol, and partakes of Sakau, but is frustrated when she hears of the "miseducation" of the Micronesian children. Finally, the traveler Is enthralled by the similarities between the Chuukese and the black people that she knew in the rural south. She sits for hours relishing the lagoon and watching boats speed to the outer islands. Again, however, she listens in dismay as she hears stories of the disintegration of the Chuukese extended family. As she leaves these idyllic islands, one agonizing question remains deep in the heart of the traveler. By whose standards do we judge the good life, and must we give up our identity, our cultural center, and our essence to have it, even if the definition is not our own?

The Spiritual Traveler Vol. III
New Orleans: The Essence of the Big Easy
p.w. long
ISBN: 978-4-902837-03-X

New Orleans has always been one of the traveler's favorite cities. Since she was a girl, she has loved the place. Her first memories of New Orleans are sitting on the porch of family friends and feasting on red beans and rice deep in the heart of the Ninth Ward. She has returned again and again, taking her children there so that they could experience the magic of this wonderful city.

The traveler even has a set of rituals reserved for her visits. She must stay at the St. James Hotel, a 1857 landmark, furnished in the French Indies style that she loves. Her first breakfast in the city is one of beignets and café au lait at the Café du Monde. She must have a shrimp po-boy at some time during her visit, and cannot leave the city without relishing the fried pickles from her favorite restaurant, The Praline Connection. A ride in a riverboat along the Mississippi is mandatory and $20.00 played on the quarter slot machines at Harrad's completes the list of must do's.

New Orleans has a vibrancy, an energy, a presence of spirit that cannot be defined, only experienced. Being there feels almost surreal. New Orleans is a place to eat good food, have a good time, and even engage in excesses if you must. For many people who visit, it is a time to take off the mask, to let their dark side be known. The hedonism and extreme vulgarity so often exhibited by tourists attending Mardi Gras is evidence of this. Now in the aftermath of Hurricane Katrina, the dark side of New Orleans has come to light and the mask has been removed for the world to see. The traveler takes a deeper look at New Orleans; with and without her mask, so that the city's essence can be revealed.

http://www.thespiritualtraveler.com
http://www.blueoceanpublishing.com
http://www.aoishima-research.com

blue ocean press is an imprint of Aoishima Research Institute (ARI)